THE GREAT PHARMACY ADVENTURE

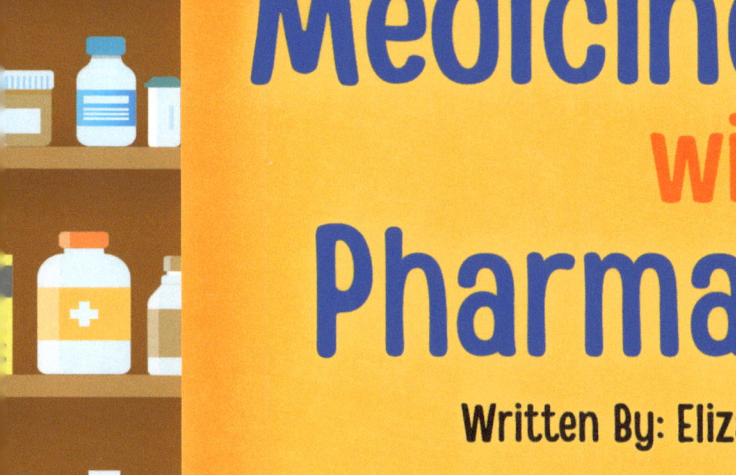

Medicine Safety
with
Pharmacist Flo

Written By: Elizabeth DeWalsche

The Great Pharmacy Adventure:
Medicine Safety with Pharmacist Flo

Copyright © 2024 by Elizabeth DeWalsche

Illustrated By: Quynh Rua

First published in 2024

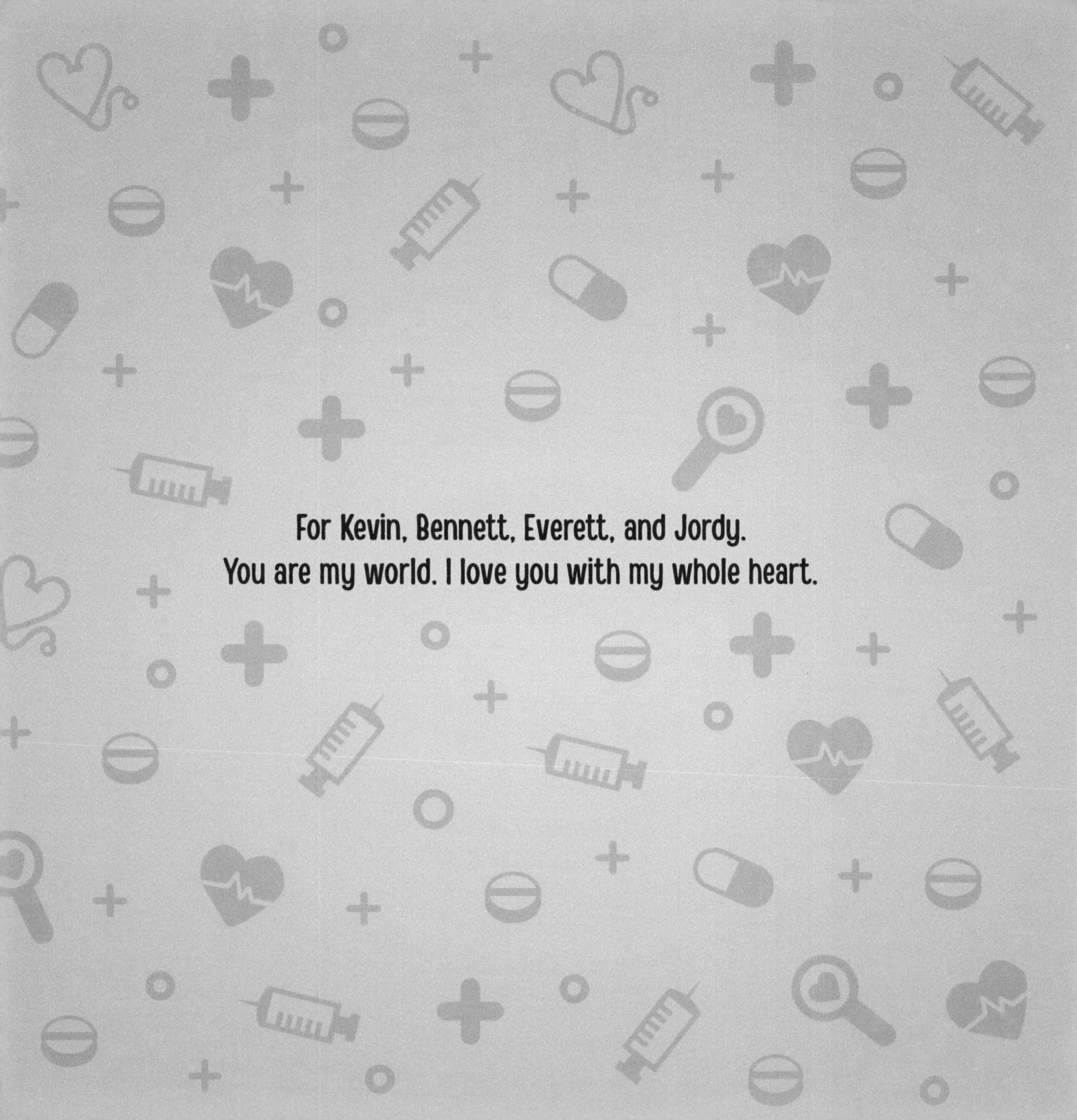

For Kevin, Bennett, Everett, and Jordy.
You are my world. I love you with my whole heart.

Parents and educators, to follow along with the book and use props to teach at home or in class, you will need these supplies:

- Two clear jars, one filled with medicine and the other filled with candy.
- A bottle of liquid medicine, a syringe, and a dosing cup.
- A prescription vial with a label.
- A syringe with a needle and a sharps container.
- A cabinet where you can practice safely storing medicine.

Once upon a time, there was a very friendly pharmacist named Flo. Flo loved her job because she helped sick people feel better. Flo also loved teaching children how to use medicine safely. One day, Pharmacist Flo decided to invite all the children in town to her pharmacy to learn about medicine safety.

When everyone arrived at the pharmacy, Flo put on her white coat and greeted everyone with a big smile. "Welcome, friends! Thank you for coming to my pharmacy to learn about medicine safety today! My name is Flo, and I am a pharmacist. Does anyone know what a pharmacist does?"

Bennett raised his hand and said, "You give people medicine to help them feel better when they are sick."

Flo nodded and said, "That's exactly right, Bennett! I help people safely get the medicine their doctor wants them to have to feel better."

Flo continued as all the children watched her, eager to learn. "Medicine can help you feel better when taken the right way, but it can be harmful if not taken correctly. That is why it is very important to learn about medicine safety and never to take medicine that doesn't belong to you or without an adult knowing." The children all nodded in understanding.

Flo walked the children over to the pharmacy shelves. On the shelves were two clear jars: one with pills in it and the other with candy in it, a medicine vial, a bottle of liquid medicine, a syringe with a needle, and a sharps container. Bella raised her hand and said, "I can't believe there are so many different types of medicines!" The children all looked at Flo with wide eyes.

Flo smiled and said, "Medicine comes in all sorts of forms. Learning about each type of medicine can help you to take medicine safely. Let's talk about each of these medicines." All the children looked at Flo, excited to learn more.

Flo held up the two clear jars. "Can anyone tell me which one of these is medicine and which one is candy?" The children looked intently at each jar considering.

Everett raised his hand and said, "It's hard to tell, but I think the one in your right hand has candy in it."

Flo said, "That's right, good job! One very important thing about medicine is that it can look like candy. That's why it's always important to ask an adult first before eating or drinking something you found lying around."

Flo put down the two jars and held up the medicine vial. She pointed to the vial lid and said, "This is a safety cap. This prevents little ones from opening up medicine when they shouldn't. If you see medicine without a lid, make sure to tell an adult right away."

Flo then pointed to the label on the medicine vial. "This label tells you who the medicine is for, what the medicine is, and how to take it. Remember to always read the label before taking medicine and never take medicine that doesn't belong to you."

Flo then held up the bottle of liquid medicine and said, "This is liquid medicine, and it must be measured correctly before taking it. Remember always to use the syringe or dosing cup that comes with it and never use a household spoon or guess how much medicine to take."

All the children practiced reading the pharmacy label and measuring out the right amount of liquid in the dosing cup. The children laughed and felt proud to measure medicine correctly.

Flo then held up the syringe and needle and asked, "Does anyone know what type of medicine this is?"

Jordy put his hand in the air and shouted, "That's a shot!"

Flo laughed and said, "Yes, that's right! Certain medicines come as shots and can be given at home by adults. Other shots, called vaccines, are usually given by a nurse, doctor, or pharmacist. After a shot or vaccine is given, it should always be put in a special container so no one can get hurt after it's given. It is very important to tell an adult right away if you find a shot outside of this special container. Make sure never to touch a needle and tell an adult where you found it. They will know how to put it into the special container safely."

"Now that we've talked about some of the different types of medicine, it is important to know where medicine should be kept. Medicine should always be locked in a safe place where little ones are not able to reach."

Flo brought all the children further into the pharmacy and showed them a cabinet where medicine could be stored safely. All the children were excited to practice putting away medicine in a safe place.

After the lesson was complete, Pharmacist Flo passed out certificates with a huge star on them to each child and said, "You are all now Medicine Safety Superstars! Thank you for coming to my pharmacy to learn about medicine safety today!"

The children all cheered and were proud of themselves for knowing how to be safe with medicines.

Medicine Safety Superstar

To continue to be a Medicine Safety Superstar, you must:

- Never take medicine without an adult knowing.
- Keep medicine stored in a safe place.
- Always tell an adult if you find medicine lying around.
- Always read the medicine label before taking it.
- Never share your medicine with others.

Reading Comprehension Questions

1. What does Pharmacist Flo teach the children about the two clear jars?

2. Why is it important to use a syringe or dosing cup when measuring liquid medicine?

3. What should you do if you find a medicine vial without a safety cap?

4. How can you tell if something is medicine or candy?

5. What are the children supposed to do if they find a needle outside of a sharps container?

6. Where can medicine be stored safely?

For poison emergencies,
call the

POISON
CONTROL
CENTER

hotline at

1-800-222-1222

or visit

Poisonhelp.org

www.ingramcontent.com/pod-product-compliance
Lightning Source LLC
Chambersburg PA
CBHW041610120626
46551CB00002B/378